Oh, the Stories I Can Tell

25 Years in the Nuisance Wildlife Control Business

Young raccoons living in someone's attic.

Jon Quint

PAGE PUBLISHING
Conneaut Lake, PA

First originally published by Page Publishing 2024

ISBN 979-8-89315-296-8 (pbk)
ISBN 979-8-89315-310-1 (digital)

Printed in the United States of America

Dedication

This book is dedicated to a member of *the Greatest Generation*, WWII Navy veteran Carleton L. Quint, a.k.a. Pop, my stepfather. A better man, you will not find. He married a widow with two kids in 1952, when I was almost 10 and my sister was 4, and became a wonderful father to both of us. I would tell him some of the tales written about in this book, and he would always get a good laugh out of them. He passed away in January of 2023 at the young age of 101. RIP, Pop!

Contents

Introduction

My adventures into the fascinating, disturbing, funny, sad, happy, wonderful world of nuisance wildlife work began with honeybees in 1986. Yeah, I know, it was a strange beginning, but follow me here. It will make sense. I have had a garden for as far back as I can remember. I have hunted, fished, and/or trapped fur for most of my life going back to the early 1950s. I have always seemed to have a strong connection to the natural world.

That year (1986), I saw a beginner's beekeeping kit in my annual Burpee seed catalog. I said to my wife, "I have to try this," since I had always been fascinated by honeybees since I was a kid. My cousin and I used to watch them work the clover flowers on my parents' front lawn, and we used to try to follow them back to their hive. We never had any luck, but probably would have wound up at one of those white boxes someone else was keeping them in, so I ordered it, and about a week later, I received the equipment and set it up. I waited for the bees. This was near the end of April. Oh, the agony of waiting. I was so excited to be doing this. They finally arrived in early June. They came in a four-sided wooden box with window screening on the other two sides. Inside was a cluster of about three thousand honeybees surrounding a small cage that contained their queen. I opened the box and installed the bees in the hive. Installing the bees involved opening the container they came in and dumping most of the bees into the hive. The package is then placed on the ground near the hive entrance, and the remaining bees will leave and enter the hive. I then removed the queen's cage, a miniature version of the bee package with small holes on both ends. One hole has a cork in it (that is the hole used to put the queen and some workers in when it is readied for shipment), and the other has some hardened "candy" in it. When placed in the hive, the worker bees in the hive chew the candy out, while getting used to her pheromones, and release her into the hive. My beekeeping career had begun.

Package of honeybees.

Every year, the number of hives I had increased until I reached about sixty-two hives about seven to eight years into my beekeeping adventure. One of the things I did as a beekeeper was to remove hives, live, from unwanted spots such as soffits of houses, old barrels, unused sheds, etc. This would get me free bees (and a little income), that I could use to start new hives or pump up the population of some hives that were not doing too well. I will not get into how they are removed because this book is not about honeybees. It is just to show how my pest and wildlife control business started.

In late summer, I would start getting phone calls from people saying they had bees in their (stick a location here), and could I come remove them. Well, I would go to check it out and find out that they were yellow jackets, a member of the wasp family, and of no use to a beekeeper, since they are carnivorous and do not make honey or beeswax. I would have to tell the people that I could not help them because they were no use to me, and I was not licensed to kill them. It only took a few of these calls for that little light bulb to go off in my head and say, "Well, dummy, let's go get your license." So I approached our Department of Environmental Protection, which issued the licenses, and signed up for the tests. You had to take a written test, and if you passed, you got two chances to pass an oral exam to get the license. If you failed the written or the oral, you had to start all over again, with a new fee, of course. I failed the written the first time. Not by much, but I had gone in cold and had not really studied, simply because I did not know where to study or how. So I did a little research and found out what was really involved, got some material to study, and went back to take the written test again. Passed with excellence this time, and now onto the oral. Talk about nerves and butterflies. I had no idea what to expect. I went to Hartford, Connecticut, on the day of the exam, took the oral, and totally blew it. I found out later that nine out of ten people fail the oral exam on the first try. I took it again and passed. Now this gave me a license to do general and rodent pest control (ants, wasps, hornets, cockroaches, clothes moths, mice, rats—every insect except termites). Termites was a separate license that I never got. After I had been building the business for a couple of years, I got a phone call from a gentleman who was my supervisor in a factory where I used to work doing production control work. He had gotten into pest control when the plant we worked at closed. I had gotten a new job but was laid off from that one after about ten years and then was out of work for a year and a half before I got another job. Four months later, I got laid off again. I said to myself, "Not doing that again!" I had been doing odd jobs, delivering newspapers, and collecting unemployment insurance. So when I decided to start a pest control business, I had free time to build the business. It took about three years before it got to the point where I could make a decent living at it and could stop the part-time jobs and the newspaper deliveries.

My former supervisor suggested to me that I should add nuisance wildlife control to my business. He said it would not make me a living completely but would be a nice add-on to the rest of my business. Well, since I had a good history with wildlife and the natural world, I thought, "Why not?" Of course, this was another license and another fee. I went to Hartford again, took the test, and was told later that I got 100 percent on it, and I was the first person to ever do that. I now have my NWCO (nuisance wildlife control operator) license. My background had paid off.

This book is going to get you into the world I lived in for over twenty-five years. It will give you information about the various animals, their place in nature, their biology, and my experiences with them. One thing that I always had a gripe with was the total lack of knowledge and common sense about wildlife in the general population. I hope people will buy this book and use it as a source of knowledge and a research tool when they run across a wildlife sighting, problem, or mysterious noises in their attic. It is especially important that children be exposed to this book and get ideas for class projects. There will be one chapter for each animal.

Disclaimer

I live in Western Connecticut, so this book will be about my experiences in Southern New England and its associated wildlife. There are different animals in other parts of the country that I have no life experience with. The processes and equipment needed to deal with them may be the same as what I used or something completely different.

This book will encompass animals that I dealt with on a regular basis. There are some animals that I have either never dealt with or require additional licensing that I never got or applied for. Animals I have never dealt with include rabbits and chipmunks. Rabbits, I just never got a call for them. Chipmunks like certain habitats, and because of their reproductive capacity, the only way to get rid of them is to change the habitat around your house. This can result in significant costs depending on your circumstances. They do not do any major damage, and I suggest just enjoying watching them run about in their daily routines. If you have patience, you can train them to take peanuts out of your hand. I have done this.

Beaver requires a special permit from CT DEEP, and I just never got those because I got very few calls for them. Foxes, I would get maybe one call every two years or so, and again they require a special permit. I did one job for them. A one-way door to get them out from under someone's deck. One-way doors are allowed for foxes without the special permit. Coyotes were a special course you had to take to get permitted for them, and because I rarely got calls for them, I never bothered to take that course. Some other rarely seen animals include fishers, porcupines, weasels, and muskrats. Again, I never got calls for them

Larger animals like deer and black bear are done by biologists from CT DEEP. These cannot be handled by individuals like me.

I have also received calls for feral cats. These are considered domestic animals and not wildlife, so my license did not cover them. There is nothing I could do with them, even though sometimes they can become a major problem.

Per Connecticut state regulations, animals that are vectors for rabies, such as raccoons, skunks, and foxes, if captured, must be released on the property they are caught on or euthanized. I did my best over the years to avoid euthanizing any animals, but sometimes, that could not be avoided, unfortunately.

Mice and rats are part of the pest control side of my business and are not considered wildlife for the purposes of this book and will not be discussed here.

Here We Go!

Spring is a time that will mean animal babies all over the neighborhood. Baby birds with their mouths wide open in nests, waiting to be fed. Pollywogs swimming in vernal pools. Baby raccoons, skunks, foxes, possums, etc. living huddled together in hollow logs and trees, in old stone walls, under sheds, decks, and raccoons in chimneys. They could be at your house. You are sitting at your kitchen table late one morning in late May, drinking coffee and watching the new leaves on the trees and the new green grass filling in after the winter. Suddenly you see it! An adult raccoon is walking across your back lawn. It's daylight, and they are nocturnal. They are not supposed to be out in daylight. Something must be wrong. It must be sick. Could it be rabid? Relax. You are right. They should not be out during daylight and normally are not, but out back is that old dead tree with the hollowed-out area near the top. You have been planning to have it taken down but have not gotten around to it. Well, inside that tree are four baby raccoons about four weeks old, and they are hungry and getting hungrier every day. The days are getting longer, the nights shorter, and the babies need to be fed, so the mother is forced to stay out during some daylight to get enough food for her kids. A normal nocturnal animal seen outside in daylight during April, May, June, and into July is not a major cause for concern if they are acting normally. It is that kids will be kids, and they need a constant supply of food. Always use caution around wild animals, but in this case, enjoy watching something you normally do not see.

Gray Squirrels

"Rats with bushy tails?" I have heard them described that way. These are the critters you see hopping around your lawn looking for nuts and various other things they eat. These critters made up about 1/4 of all the wildlife I did. They nest in hollow tree trunks or nests made of twigs and leaves in the branches of trees. Occasionally, they will get into people's attics or other places they should not be. Their population rises and falls from year to year depending mostly on the previous fall's nut crop. They feed mostly on nuts: acorns, hickory, beechnuts, and butternuts. During the summer, they will also feed on maple seeds, berries, mushrooms, and corn from a farmer's field or your home garden. The nuts are what they store for winter food, which is why the year's nut crop is so important to what the population will be the following year. Poor nut crops will result in a lot starving over the winter or not breeding that year. They breed in the December to January period and give birth in late February to early April. Some will have a second litter in the July–August period. They give birth to two to seven young that are hairless and helpless. They are weaned and become independent at about nine weeks (about two months) old. There is also a black color phase that is becoming a little more common every year. Gray squirrels can be extremely destructive, especially if they get into an attic or garage where birdseed or pet food may be stored. If they get into an attic, they can destroy wiring by chewing on it and start a fire. They will also rearrange the insulation to their liking. They are notorious chewers. If they want to get into something, wooden boards will not stop them. They will chew right through them. They can access your attic through a rotten or missing board in the house's soffit, or one of their favorite access points is the louver at the ends of the house that are for attic ventilation. They will chew through the wooden slats and push through the window screening on the inside or push through an aluminum louver. The best way to prevent this is to install tough 1/2" by 1" welded wire fencing over the outside of the louvers. Another spot they use to access attics is the spot where one roof meets another. This is what I did, but you must make sure that they are out of the attic when you do it, or you find them in your lap someday when you are watching television. However the squirrel is getting in, a solution can be found. I always tried to set up a plan so that I knew I was catching the offending squirrel and not just another squirrel that happened to be passing by. The key to a successful job was to force the squirrel(s) into your trap. This is accomplished by finding the squirrels' entry point and setting up equipment so that all squirrels are removed, and you know you have them all. I did this by putting fencing over their entry point and then cutting two square holes in that fencing. To one I would attach a one-way door going in and then a one-way door *trap* coming out. This way, if the squirrel is out when I set it up, it has access to its nesting spot without chewing a new hole to get back in. The next time it came out, it would be forced into the trap.

No bait is required. Once caught, the squirrels can be relocated. Care must be taken to make sure baby squirrels are not left behind. This is done by understanding their breeding cycle. If there was chance that unweaned babies were in there and the area could not be accessed from inside, I would recommend that the customer give it a few weeks for the babies to grow up before we did the job.

Pictured on the left is the one-way door and on the right is an example of a one-way door trap. The only difference is the one-way door is open at both ends and the trap, only at the entry end.

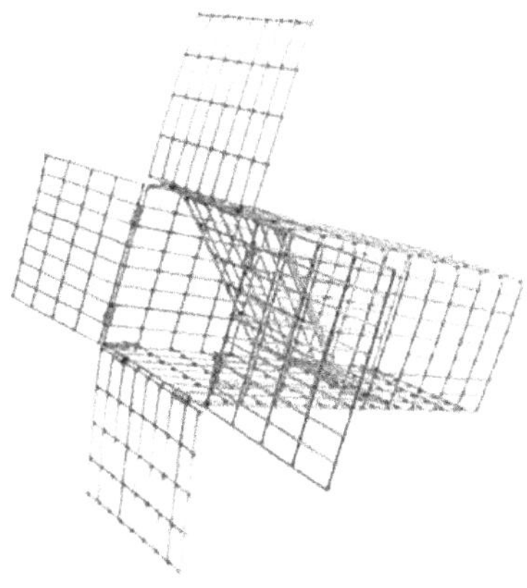

One-way door.

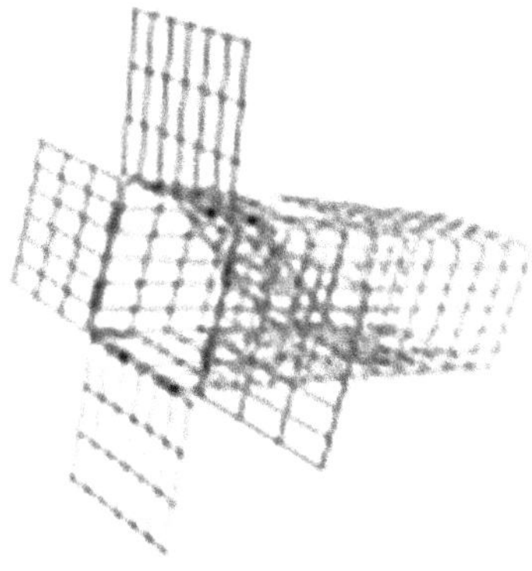

One-way door trap.

Now when I started this business, I had my knowledge of wildlife but knew nothing about removing it from unwanted places. I did not have a mentor, so I was going to learn from the old school of hard knocks. My first job naturally was a squirrel in the attic. I showed up at the guy's house and quickly found where the squirrel was getting in. It was getting in where the front porch roof met the house roof. Now what do I do? Well, I set up a baited trap, checked it the next morning, and nothing. Okay, let us try two baited traps. Again, nothing. Now I put up some bird spike material, which are closely attached wires about four inches long used to prevent birds from landing on any given area. This did not faze the squirrel at all. I went back to the traps again. Next morning? I got him! He was lying dead near the house on the front lawn. He had been hit by a car and died trying to get back to the attic. How did I know that was the offending squirrel? The homeowner said the noises stopped. I covered the hole with fencing and called it a job. Talked to the homeowner after. I told him about my lack of experience, and he was my first job, and I was going to chalk it up to learning and would not charge him for it. We both had a good laugh about it.

Over my twenty-five-year career, I did over two hundred squirrel jobs of various problems. The one-way door trap I have pictured is about 5" × 5" × 16" and has held as many as seven squirrels at once. The entire family! Packed in there like sardines and all very healthy. Unfortunately, if you do these jobs during the winter, sometimes if you catch a squirrel late in the day, then it will die in the trap overnight, so I always tried to check myself or have the homeowner check the trap just before dark, and if I had caught one or more, I would bring them home, put them in my basement overnight, and release them in my backyard the next morning. I feed the birds so there was always ample food for them until they got settled in my neighborhood, with a stern warning that if they get into my attic, they will be going to the great oak tree in the sky.

Gray squirrels in a trap.

The process I have explained here for getting rid of squirrels will apply to other animals as well. It is just the size of the trap that will differ. We will get into that as we go along.

What can sometimes be needed for squirrel work.

Another problem I encountered quite often, especially in winter, is someone gets a squirrel running around inside the house. These are normally ones that have fallen down a fireplace chimney, into the fireplace, and escaped into the house. Sometimes they will fall down the chimney and get stuck above a closed damper. These are normally pregnant females looking for a place to build a nest to raise their young. They have no way out now. The flue liner of the chimney is too smooth so they cannot climb out, and the closed damper will prevent them from getting down into the fireplace. If they do not receive any help, they will die there. It can be tricky getting a squirrel that is in a fireplace, because you must have free access to the fireplace doors or screen a little bit to get at the squirrel, which also opens a spot for the squirrel to escape into the room. This also applies to other animals as well, as we will see.

I was about 90 percent effective at getting the squirrels without them escaping into the room, but one little guy really did a job. He had been in the chimney for a while and was black with soot. I had opened the fireplace glass doors a little, but he got away from me just as I was about to grab him with my gloved hand. The room had a pair of French doors across the room that I had opened, so he could get out if he got away from me. When he escaped, he took a sharp right turn and ran up the arm of a beautiful white couch, across the back of it and down the other arm, and then out the door. Black footprints all along his voyage along the couch. When I left, the owner was going to get the upholstery cleaner.

Now my favorite gray squirrel story. About fifteen to twenty years ago, around 1:00 p.m., I got called to a law office in Waterbury, Connecticut, for a squirrel running around the office. When I arrived, the squirrel was missing in action. The office was divided by those fabric-covered cubicle walls most of us are familiar with. I found the squirrel hiding in a corner behind the cubicle walls that had been set up against the existing wall, leaving about a 4" gap between the cubicle wall and the building wall. I set up a trap at the end of the wall and put several cardboard boxes on top of it to prevent the squirrel from jumping over the trap. I took a pole I had and went to the corner, and from over the top of the wall, I started poking the squirrel along toward the trap. I got him about halfway along the wall, and suddenly, he took off like a shot and ran right into the trap and set it off, but he turned in the trap and headed out so fast that when the trap door came down, it caught him by the tail, but he was outside the trap. I had my heavy-duty gloves on and managed to get a hold of him so I could get him back into the trap. I held him with one hand while I tried to open the trap with my other hand. It is hard to open the trap with one hand, and during my struggles, the squirrel got away from me. Instantly, he vanished. I searched the office for another half hour and could not find him. I told the woman from the law office that I was working with that I would have to set and bait the trap and leave it overnight. However, after his experience with the trap, I had my doubts that he would go anywhere near it, but I set it, baited it, and headed home.

About 5:00 p.m., I got a call from the woman at the office. We had caught the squirrel in the trap! I was totally surprised! He must have been in there for a while and was mighty hungry. I went back to Waterbury, got paid for the job, and came home with the squirrel.

When I got home, I took him out behind the house and let him go by my woodpile, which is near the back door. By now, my wife had gotten home from work and was inside preparing supper. I went into the house, washed up, and sat down to eat. Now you need to know that we eat on TV trays in the living room while we watch the news. As I was eating, I suddenly heard a squirrel chattering right between my chair and the end table next to it. I slowly peeked over the edge of the chair, and there was the squirrel sitting right next to it. Now the critter is inside *my* house. I motioned to my wife and slowly got out of my chair and went out to my truck to get my hoop net. This is a net on the end of a pole that has a cable running through the handle so the top of the net can be pulled closed. I set up the net next to the front side of the chair and asked my wife to take a broom and push the squirrel toward the net. Sure enough, he ran right into the net. I quickly pulled the cable and closed the net. As I turned around to head out the door, I noticed the squirrel was hanging on the outside of the net. He dropped off and headed down the hall toward the bed-rooms. I started looking for him again and found him hiding behind the waste basket in the bathroom. I shut the bathroom door and told my wife we should finish dinner, clean up, and then deal with the squirrel. After this was done, I went back into the bathroom with the net, caught the squirrel, and this time I flipped the net over figuring the first time, he may have squeezed out through the top, which does not close completely tight. As I got out into the hallway, I noticed he was hanging off the outside of the net again. He dropped off and ran back into the bathroom behind the wastebasket again. It was now obvious that the net pole was not going to work, so I went out to the truck and got my grasper, a tool that allows me to grasp and pick up an animal from a distance. I grasped the squirrel and headed outside. I made sure the door was shut tight and went out to the woodpile. I let the squirrel go, and he ran up a nearby tree trunk to a height of about my eye level. I turned around and headed back into the house.

The next thing I know is the squirrel is hanging on to my right leg between my ankle and knee. Okay, this is enough! I grabbed the squirrel with the grasper, went into the garage, and put him back in the trap. He spent the night in the trap in the garage, and the next morning we took a ride to Litchfield (about fifteen miles away), and I let him go to the White Memorial Foundation, in Litchfield, Connecticut, which is a four-thousand-acre wildlife sanctuary. I never saw him again, but that night, I woke up in the middle of the night, and I just had to sit up and check the bottom of the bed to make sure he was not sitting at the foot of the bed looking at me.

I have spent many an hour chasing squirrels around houses. Some ended very quickly, and others lasted an hour or more. It was good exercise for me and for the squirrels.

Usually, these squirrels get in the house by falling down the chimney and getting in through the fireplace.

Interesting things can happen sometimes! I received a phone call from a gentleman years ago, here in Woodbury, who told me he thought he had a squirrel in his chimney in his old colonial home. He had heard noises early in the morning but had not heard anything after that. It was an old house, so I told him his chimney might have a flue liner in it which could prevent the squirrel from climbing out, and he might get out because there was no flue liner and only the stones in the original chimney, which it could easily climb. I told him to call me after he got home from work if he heard any more noises. About 7:00 p.m., he called and said his wife had heard noises again. I told him I would come over the next morning and get it out for him.

When I got there, I discovered that there were two fireplaces back-to-back, on an interior wall, which shared a common chimney, so the critter was going from one side to the other.

This was going to be difficult. If I set up at one fireplace, the critter would go to the other side. I was debating what to do when the customer said to me, "If we light a fire on this side, won't that drive him to the other side?" Customers are smart. I never thought of that. So that is what we did. We lit a fire on one side and as we were watching, the customer went into the other room, and I heard him say, "Oh, it's a—"

It was a screech owl. I picked him out of the fireplace and took him outside. I let him go, and he flew about fifty feet and fell into the snow. I went over, picked him up, and put him in a cage trap. He was exhausted and dehydrated from about twenty-four hours in the chimney. I called a wildlife rehabilitator, explained the situation, and she said to bring him over. I delivered the poor little guy, and she said she would give him some raw hamburger and fluids and release him in a couple of days. A nice, interesting call that ended simply fine.

The picture is him sitting on the rehabilitator's hand.

Screech owl in fireplace.

One little trick I learned, when dealing with squirrels in a chimney that cannot be removed from inside, is to go up on the roof and drop a piece of heavy rope (at least an inch in diameter) down the chimney, thereby giving the squirrel something to grab on to and climb out.

Red Squirrels

Red squirrels are not as common in western Connecticut as gray squirrels are, and they are normally associated with evergreen trees since their main source of food is the seeds inside the "pine" cones. They will eat bird eggs, berries, and fruits if they are available. They are reddish, with a white belly, and a very distinctive white eye ring. They are about twelve inches long and about half the size of gray squirrels. They nest in ground burrows, hollow trees, or nest in trees that they construct out of twigs and leaves in the crouch of tree branches. They breed in late winter/early spring, and after a gestation period of about five to six weeks (about one and a half months), they give birth to three to six blind and helpless young. After five to six weeks (about one and a half months), the young start going outside with the mother and will stay with her throughout the summer.

Trapping red squirrels is the same as for gray squirrels. Most of the jobs I did on them were routine, but one does stick out in my mind both at the expense of the squirrel and me. I got called to a house in a neighboring town. The female caller explained to me that a red squirrel had fallen down their fireplace chimney and escaped into their living room. They had chased it around for a while, trying to get it outside, and now they had it cornered in a bedroom with the door closed and a towel under the door so it could not escape under the door. When I arrived, they showed me the room. I had my heavy-duty biteproof gloves on, my grasping tool, a cage trap to put him in, and a handheld net. I casually entered the room and closed the door behind me. I did a quick survey of the room and found there was not much in it. A wall bookcase on one end with a few books in it, a bed, one dresser, and a nightstand. I said to myself, "This should be fairly easy." Little did I know. That was the night I found out just how fast and sneaky red squirrels can be. I chased him around the bedroom for over an hour. Thought I had him many times, but it was not to be. I finally got him in the net, put him in the trap, and took a rest. I honestly do not know who was more winded and exhausted, me or the squirrel. Took the little guy outside and let him go and advised the homeowner to get a chimney cap put on.

Flying Squirrels

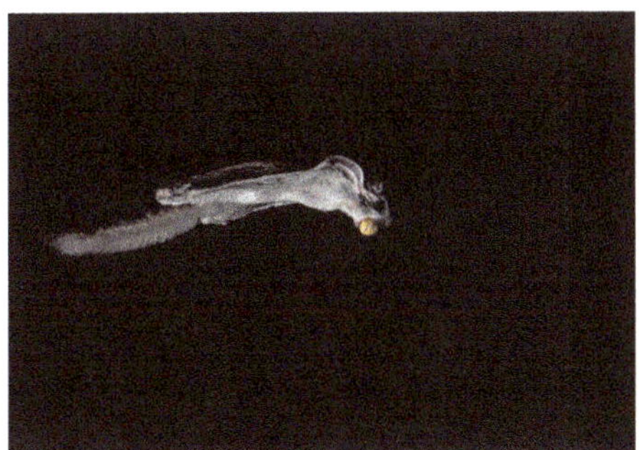 

These little critters are about the size of a chipmunk and have a large flap of skin between their front and hind legs, called a patagium. When they jump off a roof or tree limb, they put their legs out and become little gliders. The fur on their tail is flattened top to bottom, and this is used as a rudder to steer when they are airborne and as an air brake when they are about to land. Unlike other species of squirrels (gray and red), which are seen hopping around during the day, flying squirrels are nocturnal. They are out at night. They can be quite noisy when they leave in the evening and when they return just before daylight. Most people do not hear them leave (right around dark) because usually people are active then, talking, the TV is on, and supper is being prepared, but in the morning (just before it starts getting light out) is when they are heard coming back from a night out, because the house is usually quiet at that time.

They are omnivorous, eating about anything. They will eat seeds, nuts, berries, fruit, mushrooms, carrion, bird eggs, etc. Occasionally, they will come into bird feeders at night; if you move very slowly, they can be approached quite closely. They are preyed on by owls, snakes, raccoons, and house cats.

They mate in March and April and give birth during April and early May to two to six young. The young will start going out with the adults at about six weeks (about one and a half months), so no exclusion work should be done until the end of June at the earliest; otherwise, the young will remain behind to die.

I have chased many of these guys around in houses. They will climb up drapes, and then just as you are about to grab them, they jump off and glide across the room. Some you catch right away, and other times they will lead you on the hunt for an hour or more. Ones that get into a house usually arrive by way of the fireplace chimney like gray squirrels and like them, will die in there unless rescued if the damper is shut.

I did a flying squirrel job in Bethlehem. I set up a one-way door trap at the obvious entry point (hole chewed in the soffit of the roof). The guy called me the next morning to inform me that I had four or five in the trap (it turned out to be seven). Flying squirrels are nocturnal, so they are always caught overnight. I drove up there, swapped out the trap, and brought them home to release in my back-yard. I let them go by opening the trap and putting it against a tree trunk, and they ran out and up the tree. Well, six of them left and scampered up the tree, but the seventh one came out and just sat there, so my wife decided to see how close she could get. I guess its back hurt and decided to stick around and see if someone would give it a back rub! My wife did! She gave a back rub to a flying squirrel!

Striped Skunk

Skunks are nocturnal. They are omnivores, feeding on just about anything, but their main diet is insects—caterpillars, grasshoppers, beetles, crickets, etc. They will also feed on worms, crayfish, and other noninsect arthropods. In winter and early spring, they will supplement their diet with mice, voles, bird eggs, and young bird chicks. They will feed on bees and are notorious for digging up yellow jackets in the ground and consuming all the jackets and the eggs and larvae. I have lost several jobs over the years to skunks. I would tell a customer that I would be out the next day to take care of their yellow jacket nest in the ground, only to get there and find a hole in the ground and some scraps of paper nesting material. A skunk had beat me to it!

Skunks are polygamous, with the males mating with several females in late February to early March. The females give birth to an average of five to six kits. The young's eyes do not open for about three weeks, they are weaned at about six weeks (about one and a half months) and will start accompanying the female out of the den, and they are mature and on their own at about the age of ten weeks (about two and a half months).

I went to do a carpenter ant job here in Woodbury. I checked in with the customer, told him what I was going to do, and went to the truck to get my equipment. As I started toward the back of the house, I noticed they had an in-ground swimming pool in the backyard. As I got a little closer, I noticed something in the pool. It was a young skunk, about eight weeks old, that had fallen in on one of his first trips out of the nest with his mom and his siblings. The poor little guy appeared to be skunk paddling in slow motion. He was going just fast enough to keep his head above water. I have no idea how long he had been there, but he was obviously extremely exhausted. I went and told the customer what was going on and asked him if he might have a 2 × 6 or 2 × 8 that I could slide into the pool to give him something to crawl out on. He said he did not have one, but he had a long-handled net that was used to clean stuff out of the pool. So I took that to the pool, extended it all the way out (about 15' long), placed it under the skunk, scooped him gently out of the pool, and placed him on the lawn. He stood there for a minute, then made a halfhearted attempt to shake himself off, but you could tell he decided he should just rest for a while. I kept my eye on him and proceeded to close the net handle. As I was putting it back, I noticed the classic strong skunk smell. I turned around, and the little guy was gone, but to show his gratitude at being rescued, he had sprayed in the net while he was being lifted out of the pool. Nobody got sprayed, but the backyard was stunk up good for a while. You are welcome, little skunk!

A regular customer of mine had a little shed outside that he kept his garbage pails in. Something was digging underneath to get inside the shed. I looked at it and could not tell right away whether something was digging in to get the garbage or was living under the shed. I called the customer (who was in California on vacation) and told him we could put exclusion fencing around the shed to prevent further problems and leave one spot open so we could put a trap there and catch the culprit. The hole appeared too small to be from a raccoon or woodchuck, but there was no skunk odor around either. This was very puzzling.

I got there that morning and saw that the hole was still there and was still about the same size. I opened the shed and began to look around. All the garbage had been picked up, so all the pails were empty. I looked in one and then grabbed the side of the second one. I peeked inside. There at the bottom was an adult skunk, sitting there. Surprised me a little, but once I composed myself, I carried the pail to the edge of his lawn and released the skunk. Neither it nor I were any worse for the wear, but I have no idea how long it was in there, but it was not there the other day when I checked. It fell in looking for food and could not get out.

I finished by putting in the fencing. No need to set a trap. The culprit had gotten caught in the garbage pail. Another successful job completed.

I got a call in mid-July about a family of skunks living under the front porch at a three-family house in Waterbury. I got to the address, looked, and found an obvious hole under the front porch. I set two traps and left. The following morning, I got a call from the owner that I had caught the mother skunk in one of the traps, a young one in the other trap, and there were four young ones wandering around the outside of the trap the mother was in. Oh, boy, since baby skunks have their arsenal fully loaded when they start coming out with the mother, it looked like I had a problem. I got to the job, and as I walked up toward the traps, the four young ones ran back under the porch. Whew, that problem was solved for the moment. I set two more traps, and the following morning, I had all four young in the two traps.

Opossum

Opossums are the only marsupials native to North America. They breed in early March and have a gestation period of only about two weeks and have litter of up to nine. The young, when born, are naked, blind, and about the size of a bean seed. They crawl only a few inches up to the mother's pouch, crawl in, and attach themselves to a teat. If there are more young than teats, the ones who have no teat to attach themselves to will perish. They are independent at about one hundred days (about three and a half months) old. Possums may have a second litter later in the summer. Possums are omnivorous with their diet but have a fondness for ticks. Their body temperature runs lower than most other animals, so they do not carry rabies because its virus is very susceptible to body temperatures and cannot live in a possum.

I got a call from a woman who told me she had a possum in her garage. I informed her I would not be able to make it to her house until the next day. She was fine with that. I told her she might try leaving a trail of dog or cat food out the open garage door and then go shut the door when she went to bed. The possum should have left by then for its evening foraging. She called me back later and said she chickened out and did not want to go into the garage.

When I showed up the next morning, I found two garage doors with a regular door next to them with passage into the garage and stairs up to the house. I went in through the regular door and checked under the stairs, and there was the possum looking at me. *Piece of cake*, I thought and went to get my heavy gloves and hoop pole. I came back in, went under the stairs, and the possum was gone! So I started the search, looking everywhere. I came to the guy's workbench and pulled out a box of rags that had been rounded out in the center and rags piled up around that center area for a nice little bed. Few possums have that kind of five-star hotel to sleep in.

I continued the search and could not find him anywhere. I was about to give up when I saw him under a dresser that was in the garage. I poked around under there to get him to move because I could not get him with the hoop pole under there. Finally, he moved and disappeared again! Now where was he? I went back to the workbench and saw the tail sticking out of the box of rags. He got tired of my BS and went back to bed! I grabbed his tail, pulled the box out a little, and got him behind the head with my other hand and carried him out the door. Of course, the husband had to take the obligatory photo of me holding him before I let him go. The photo must have been good because he (the possum) had his mouth open, looking all vicious! He was a little undersized, so I assumed he was one that had been born the past spring and had not reached full adult size yet. I let him go at the side of the garage, and he ran around the corner of the house and through the lattice work surrounding their deck. I told them he would be fine there and would not cause any problem.

One of my more humorous episodes with possums took place at a carpet store we had here in my hometown, Woodbury, Connecticut. The owner called me and told me he had a family of possums living in his warehouse next to the showroom. I stopped in and the owner took me to the warehouse and showed me what was going on. He had seen it, and there were droppings around the area. It was May, so the fact he had seen what he thought was five young on her back did not surprise me. I set a trap, and knowing that mother possums carry their young around on their back (when they get too big for the pouch), I was hopeful I could catch the whole family in one shot. I came back the next morning, and sure enough, there she was in the trap with four youngsters on her back.

This is their actual picture:

Okay, so she has four. Where is number 5? We started the search. Now carpet is rolled up on cardboard tubes and stacked that way so you can look at the ends of each roll, but there were close to fifty rolls in there so this would take a little time. Finally found it about halfway through the stack of rolls. It was in the back of a tube in a roll, looking at me. Now how do we get it out? Fortunately, we could easily get on the back side of the rolls, so I asked the owner if he had a long pole of some sort. He said he did, so I asked him to crumple up paper of some sort, put it in the tube, and then slowly push it toward me. I would have a trap at the end of the roll. He could push the youngster right into the trap. Sounds like a great idea, right? Well, that is how it was supposed to happen, but in the real world, we have that guy of "Murphy's law" fame (if anything can go wrong, it will) always seeming to be in operation. The young possum was much smaller than the opening of the trap, so naturally he got away. Now here I am running around the parking lot with my pole net trying to capture him. Well, it took a little while, but I finally caught him and put him in the rap with his mother and siblings. Case closed and the relocation accomplished without incident.

Bats

Bats leave their summer roosts (your attics, louvers, shutters, or soffits) for their winter hibernation in late fall, early winter. Relax, not everyone has bats! Bat exclusion can then be done without worrying about having to get the bats out first (98 percent of the time that is true). On a rare occasion, you may get one macho male bat who thinks he can overwinter in his summer roost. Those that attempt it normally die over the winter. Once bats leave, we can go over the house and close any other entry points, so when the bats return in the spring, they cannot get back in. It is much less expensive doing it this way than having to get the bats out first. And much less work for us.

Bats are nature's pest control. They fly at night and feed on insects while flying. They locate the insects by using echolocation. They send out a sound that reflects off the insect and bounces back to them, letting them know exactly where that insect is. It is like the sonar used by submarines. They feed on moths and mosquitoes. I have read that they can consume up to six hundred mosquitoes per hour.

We did a job in Roxbury, where the customer had bat droppings accumulating on the patio under the louvers (the slatted vents for the attic) of his house. We put up the ladder, climbed up, and checked. I did not know if the bats were living in the louvers, or if the louver screening had failed, and they were in the attic. No bats in that one, screening was intact, so we sprayed the live wasp nest we found, removed all the old wasp nests, and covered the louver with hardware cloth. Now to the other end of the house, put up the ladder, and along with the wasp nests, were two big brown bats hanging on the screen under the louver slats. Screening on that one was intact, too. It was a little chilly out, so the bats were a little lethargic. When I shooed them out, they did not fly. They just opened their wings and parachuted to the ground. We picked them up with gloved hands and placed them in the sunshine on a stone wall (see photos). In a short while, they had warmed to the point where they warmed up and flew away.

Bat warming on stone wall.

I went back up the ladder, cleaned out the wasp nests, and installed hardware cloth. Another successful job!

Many times, I would get phone calls in the middle of the night from people totally freaked out because "I have a bat flying in my house."

Understandable reaction from someone who only knows all the old wives' tales about bats. If you have a bat flying in your house, there is a good chance that you will have a bat colony somewhere in your attic or elsewhere. About 95 percent of my "bat flying in the house" calls came in August. Since bats give birth in early June,

August is when baby bats first start flying. They do not know the ins and outs of their roost, so they fly around, get lost, and can wind up in the living area of the house.

About ten to twelve years ago, bats started being infected with "white nose syndrome." It is a fungal disease that has devastated bat populations across much of the country. Up to 90 percent of some bat species have been lost. It affects them in their winter hibernation, a white growth appears on their face and wings. The fungus does not directly kill them, but it irritates them, so they awaken from hibernation, are hungry, and fly out looking for food. None is available at that time of the year, so they use up body fat and do not survive the winter.

Bats typically are terribly slow reproducers, having only one youngster per year. This is one reason white-nose syndrome had been so devastating.

Since bats are extremely beneficial as nature's pest control, please, please do not kill them. They are desperately needed.

Raccoons

Raccoons breed in February and March and give birth to typically four young in early to mid-May. They are blind and helpless at birth. After thirty to forty days, they begin leaving the nest with the mother and in three to four months, begin foraging on their own. They are true omnivores, eating basically anything they find. They will inspect their food, but don't wash it as portrayed in many stories. Over the years, I found that the best bait for trapping them is Dunkin Donuts munchkins and/or marshmallows with honey drizzled over them.

My stepson (Matt) and I went to Roxbury to check out a house that was having a "mysterious noises in the attic" issue. Could be raccoons, mice, flying squirrels, or gray or red squirrels. As we inspected the house, the homeowner showed us a picture of a raccoon that another pest control company had trapped several weeks ago on the roof, right where it had been getting into the attic. Okay, that eliminates raccoons!

We found several spots where critters could be accessing the attic. We decided to go into the house and check out the attics, or at least Matt could. I am getting too old for that, especially in this heat. There were several distinct parts of the attic to check. Matt went into a couple, did not stay very long because of the heat, came back down, and said that there were a lot of mice and flying squirrel droppings. He then headed for the last attic to be checked, the one near where the raccoon had been captured. Up he went, and shortly he was back down with a smile on his face. I asked him what he was smiling about, and he said that the raccoon had ripped a hole in an air-conditioning duct right next to where its nest was. It was getting too hot up there even for him, so he decided to get some AC for his nest. You will not find many animals smarter than a raccoon.

On Memorial Day weekend a number of years ago, I got a call for "mysterious" noises in the attic. The customer heard something walking and sounding like baby birds chirping. Now this was a condo complex with four units in a single building. Each unit had its own vent at the peak of the roof. I got there and looked the situation over. All four aluminum vents were bent, and I could tell that some animal, likely a raccoon, was getting into the attic. Now am I dealing with four raccoons or just one accessing all four attics?

Fortunately, I could access all the vents from one roof, so I didn't have to set up my ladder four times. I set up a cage trap at each opening. I got a call the next morning. I had a raccoon in three of the four traps. This weekend was extremely hot. Now I was faced with going into at least three of the attics to look for young raccoons because all the captured ones were nursing females. To the attic was a small opening in the bedroom closet of each unit with just a piece of push-up plywood. It was unbelievably hot up there, but the young were very vocal, so they were fairly easy to locate. I had a plastic garbage bag with me to collect them in. I had a little trouble because as I put one in and went after another, the first would crawl out of the bag. I did this for all three attics and got four, four, and three youngsters. The next day, I got a call that some noises were still being heard in one attic. I went back over there and got up in the attic where I had taken three, and sure enough, there was number 4. I missed him originally.

I left the trap at the fourth vent and never caught anything, so after a few days, I took it down, and raccoon-proofed the vent as I had done on the other three.

I think that weekend was about as close as I had ever come to getting heatstroke. God, it was hot up there!

Young raccoons in an attic.

One cute little thing baby raccoon do when they are scared is cover their eyes. I have seen it many times, and this is a picture of them doing it (not my picture).

Snakes

Snakes! Oh, the horror! I think the phobia a lot of people have about snakes goes back to the serpent in the garden of Eden from the Bible. They are not anything to fear. Despite what a lot of people think, snakes are not slimy—they are very dry to the touch.

Snakes can give birth to live young or lay eggs. It depends on the species. Snakes are incredibly good to have around. They are extremely beneficial because they eat insects, small rodents, and other small critters, and they can eat something that is a lot larger around than they are.

When we get snake calls, there is not a lot that can be done to get rid of them. There is no effective way to bait or trap them. They can be removed by carefully picking them up by the neck right behind the head, putting them in a container, and relocating. Calling someone like us usually does no good because by the time we get there, the snake will be gone. If you have one in your yard, it is because you have the three things that all living things require—food, shelter, and water. They have been around for a while, but being very secretive, you just never saw them. Snakes are harmless, even the venomous ones—the copperhead and timber rattlesnake here in Connecticut. They will just lay still until the threat has passed and will only bite if handled or feel they are cornered. You may have walked right past one in the past and never even realized it. Snakes will not chase you, and they will not attack you. They just want to be left alone to go about their business. Snakes may occupy an abandoned rodent burrow but cannot dig holes by themselves, for obvious reasons. Snakes have their place in nature like all other animals. Please *do not kill them*! Below I have posted pictures of the most common snakes in Connecticut and a little bit about each.

Whenever I got snake call, nine out of ten times, the caller would say they have a copperhead. Now Connecticut only has two venomous snakes—the copperhead and the timber rattlesnake. People would naturally think the worst, so it has to be venomous, and since it doesn't have a rattle on its tail, so it must be a copperhead. In my twenty-five years in the business, I've never seen one.

It was always a pleasure to get a call from someone who knew what they were talking about.

Copperhead.

Milk snake.

In the pictures above, I have shown the copperhead and milk snake side by side because the milk snake is most often mistaken for a copperhead. The copperhead is very uncommon and rarely seen. Note that on the copperhead, the dark bands are much wider on the side than on the back. It is a coppery color overall, and the head is much wider than the body. The milk snake's bands are the same size all the way around. If the milk snake is seen, its belly has a blue-and-white checkerboard pattern. It has a V or Y mark on the top of its head, which is only slightly wider than its body. Milk snakes occupy the typical habitat around houses and will occasionally get into a basement.

Garter snake.

Northern water snake.

The garter snake (not "garden" or "gardener" snake) is the most seen snake in Connecticut. It inhabits lawns, gardens, brush piles, stonewalls, etc. Their pattern and coloring can vary but always consists of a dark gray to blackish color, with light yellowish stripes running the length of the body. They can be easily moved along by using a broom or something similar. They do no harm.

The northern water snake is found around slow rivers, lakes, ponds, and swampy areas. It is fairly common and is *not* a water moccasin (or cottonmouth). They are nonvenomous. They feed mostly on frogs and fish but will take an occasional bird, bird egg, or rodent. While they can act aggressively, they are harmless and will leave if given the opportunity. Water moccasins are a southern snake, and their range only extends up to southern Virginia.

Ringneck snake.

The ringneck snake likes woody, rocky habitat and is very commonly found in basements. They are grayish black on the back, with a yellowish ring around the neck and a yellowish-colored belly. This is a smallish snake, with a huge one being eighteen inches long, but most are less than a foot long. They are harmless, and you might even call these guys friendly. In my experience with them, I have never seen them express anything that you could call aggression.

The garter snake, northern water snake, milk snake, and ring-neck snake are the four most seen snakes in Connecticut. There are ten other species native to our state, but those are uncommon and very rarely seen.

Snakes found in basements can be removed by putting something like a wastebasket over them and slowly pushing a piece of cardboard under the wastebasket and then taking it outside and releasing it.

I got a call from a woman in a neighboring city one fall season. She said she was just in her basement doing laundry and saw a snake about 4' long. Could I come over and get it out for her? I asked her if she had a lot of stuff in the basement because snakes are experts at hiding. She said she only had a washer and dryer. I told her I'd be right over. When I got there, I went down cellar, and sure enough, she only had a washer and dryer and no snake in sight. I looked around, tipped up the washer and dryer. Nothing! So where is this 4' snake? I saw a small pile of leaves by the Bilco door. Walked over to it and kicked at it with my foot. Out crawled a newly born garter snake (they give birth to live young in late summer early fall) about the size of a number 2 pencil. Here was the 4' monster she saw! Over the years, I have found that when I get a snake call and described as so and so feet long, it always turns out to be half that length or less.

Here is a story about a snake job I did years ago that is interesting but does not involve a native Connecticut species. I got a call from a family in a nearby town on a Saturday. Their nineteen-year-old son was away for a camping weekend, and when his mother took some clean laundry into his room, she noticed that the plywood top to his pet snake's terrarium had been pushed over. What kind of snake was it, you ask? It was a Burmese python about 8' long. The terrarium covered the entire length of one wall of his bedroom. Pythons are constrictors and are not venomous, so no worries if we should get bitten.

Burmese python.

Now the family has three dogs. Chihuahuas! Just meal size for this snake. I better find it fast. The husband helped me search. We could not find it anywhere in the house, but there was a connection to an unfinished area over the attached garage. We decided to look out there. The father had a covered Rubbermaid container and a roll of duct tape with him, and I had a four-foot grasper, a tool that allows me to grab something from a distance. We went up the stairs, and there it was, coiled up in the far corner. Okay, here we go! The snake and I made eye contact, and it was as if it said, "Okay, you want to get it on? Let's do it right now," and it started crawling right toward me! As it got closer, I had the grasper in my left hand, and I managed to grab the snake right behind its head and was able to hang on just long enough so I was able to grab him by the neck with my right hand. I had a good grip on it, and it started trying to coil its body around my arm. The strength of this snake was incredible. The husband was uncoiling it as fast as it was trying to get its body around my arm. We finally got control of it and put it in the Rubbermaid container and put the lid on. The husband used all that roll of duct tape, wrapping it around and around the container. We carried it down into the garage. As I settled with him and his wife, he said the snake was going for a long ride. I have no idea where he took it, and for all I know it might still be roaming the forest of that town.

I really doubt it could withstand our winters, though. Oh, yes, before I left, we checked, and all three Chihuahuas were present and accounted for.

Another time, I had a woman call me who lived on Plymouth lake in Plymouth, Connecticut. She had a northern water snake sunning itself on the dock by her house, and they couldn't get to her boat. Could I come and take it away? I explained to her that if I came up, I would have to charge her, and in all likelihood, it would be gone by the time I got there. She said to me, "Well, you're welcome to take our boat and paddle around the lake looking for it." I explained to her that that might be a lifetime occupation, and I might never find it. Sometimes I really wonder about people.

I had captured a milk snake on a glue board, one of the very few ways of capturing a snake. The snake crawled onto the glue board, got its head stuck, and then coiled up and got the rest of its body stuck. They can be released by dumping vegetable oil on them. It dissolves the glue, and they are free to go. As I was working on freeing his body, I failed to notice that the oil ran down toward his head. The next thing I knew was his mouth was clamped onto my index finger. Here I was, holding up my hand with the snake's head attached to my finger and the glue board and the rest of his body hanging in midair. I got a hold of his head with my other hand and freed him from my finger and the rest of the glue board, letting him go to the edge of my rear lawn.

The bite was no problem since milk snakes are not venomous and have very tiny teeth, which barely broke my skin. Just watch out for any infection as you would for any break in the skin, but it would heal up with no problem.

Woodchucks

Woodchucks, or groundhogs as they are called by some people, are a medium-sized, brown animal that digs extensive burrows in the ground. Burrows can be 20–25' long and 2–5' deep. They have two or more openings. Woodchucks feed almost entirely on vegetation, which is exactly why you do not want them in your yard if you have a flower and/or vegetable garden. They will make quick work of them.

Woodchucks are the only true hibernators in this area of the country. They go into a deep sleep, and their breathing and heartbeat slows down, and they can be a little hard to rouse from this sleep.

Woodchucks breed in February/March period and give birth to two to six young during April to mid-May. The young go off on their own when they are about eight weeks old.

Woodchuck in trap.

Woodchuck.

While I did many woodchuck jobs over the years, most of them were routine, and they were fairly easy to catch. It was just finding their burrow, setting up a cage trap, baiting it with loose leaf lettuce, and usually it would be in the trap that same day. If their burrow was under a building or any structure, I would set up the trap a little away from the structure, put two cement blocks on either side, and one over the other two. The woodchuck had to go into the trap. It had no other option. This setup was also used for raccoons, possums, etc., that might be living under a structure.

I did have one interesting job, though. The woodchuck was getting in a guy's flower garden. There was a very distinct trail leading into the garden, but it came from about 150' away. That was unusual. I could not find this one's burrow (the trail went to a huge pile of rocks covered with vegetation), so I took a shot at setting the trap near the garden and putting drops of a woodchuck lure along the trail leading back the area of its burrow. This was a long shot, and I did not have much confidence that I would catch it. I explained this to the customer, and he seemed to understand. As I drove home, I could not help thinking about the job. I do not like to leave customers with an unsolved job. When I walked into my house, my answering machine was blinking that I had a message. I listened, and it was that customer telling me that the woodchuck was in the trap!

One little note about woodchucks. They are summer animals that live underground for most of the time, so they are extremely sensitive to heat and humidity. If one is caught in a trap on a hot day, out in the sun. They can quickly die from hyperthermia. They should be relocated and released quickly or at least moved into a shady spot. This is something I asked my customers to do for me if I was not going to be available for a while.

Birds

Over the years, I have taken many birds out of attics, inside houses, chimneys, fireplaces, and woodstoves. The species that come immediately to mind are crows, robins, cardinals, blue jays, wood ducks (twice from the same house in different years), and the Cooper's hawk that crashed through a picture window and landed (unhurt amazingly) on the table where four teenage girls were playing cards. I do not know who was more terrified, the hawk or the girls. Hawk successfully captured and released, unharmed, outside. Girls were calmed down. I was not sure which had more adrenalin flowing.

I went to a house that had a bird in the attic. It was just an English sparrow, but obviously we wanted to get it out. It was in a small area that required me to crawl through an exceedingly small triangular-shaped opening to reach the area. As I went in on my belly, it was a tight squeeze, and the fiber glass insulation covered my stomach, chest, and some got down inside the front of my pants. I got the little sparrow and released him safely outside. Boy, was I glad that was the final job of the day so I could get and take a shower. That insulation is nasty stuff.

Years ago, I went to Seymour for a "fluttering and squeaking" mysterious noise in the chimney of a fireplace. That covers a lot of territory. Could be about anything.

Just a side note here. If you ever hear what you think are baby birds chirping inside your fireplace chimney during late April and May, there is a good chance you have baby raccoons in there.

I got to the house, opened the screen of the fireplace, opened the damper, and got into a position where I could look up the chimney. Shined my flashlight up the chimney and saw the problem immediately. I only saw it once before in twenty years in the business. Nothing needs to be done. The problem will resolve itself shortly. The cause of the noise was chimney swifts. These are small swallow-like birds that build mud nests on the inside of chimneys. There they lay eggs, raise their young, and when the young fledge (leave the nest), they are done for that season. The nest will eventually fall onto the damper in the fireplace and break up, causing no problem at all. They will come back year after year unless the chimney is capped, but they do no harm, so why not provide them with an untroubled home and help a species that is in decline, especially in Connecticut.

This is a photo I took looking up the chimney. You can see three young, just fledged, swifts hanging on the side of the chimney. Just above and to the left of them is the edge of their nest, attached to the inside of the chimney.

Chimney swift taken out of a woodstove during the summer.

Miscellaneous Stories

Can an Ugly Reptile Be Cute?

I think they can, especially when you see this! I went to a mouse/carpenter ant job one day during late summer, and after I finished, I was standing in the customer's driveway talking to him when we saw this on his driveway. A little background here. He has a pond out behind his house, and he tells me that every June, a big female snapping turtle comes up on his lawn and tears it all up, digging a hole to lay her eggs.

Well, the summer is over, and I guess the eggs

have hatched because this is what was in his driveway. That is a quarter next to it for a size comparison. That is how big a newly hatched snapping turtle is, and we have all seen what they grow up to be. Those forty-pound, 18" long monsters you never want to deal with! A few minutes later, the customer found another one a few feet away on his lawn. When I left, he was headed for the pond to release the little guys.

Oh, the Problem with Deer

We do not do deer. Our State Department of Energy and Environmental Protection reserves that honor for themselves. The same applies to black bears. I was at a job once (I do not remember what it was) and got talking to the owner of the house. They asked me if I did anything about deer. I said we did not do deer, but what was the problem? I thought I might be able to give them some suggestions. They said that the deer were eating their shrubs, and could they stop them by installing an "invisible fence," like those used for dogs? I was stunned. I said, "Well, yes, you probably could if you can catch the deer and put the shock collars on them."

New York, New York

I was not personally involved in this story. I heard it from the guy, a local police officer friend of mine who responded to it. Dispatch radioed the officer and told him he had just received a call from an elderly gentleman who complained he kept hearing Frank Sinatra singing "New York, New York" under the shrubs near his back door. As my friend headed toward the guy's house, he thought, *Oh, boy, will I have to call the guys in the white coats for this one?* He looked over the house as he arrived and did not see anything out of the ordinary. He got out of his cruiser, walked up to the door, and knocked. The owner, a man in his eighties, came to the door and showed the officer where he was hearing the noise. He pointed out that it was under a yew shrub next to the back porch. The officer asked if the gentleman had a rake or something like that. He got the officer a rake, and the officer started poking around under the shrub just to show the owner he was investigating the issue. Suddenly he heard it, clear as a bell, Frank singing "New York, New York." He was shocked. As he investigated further, he discovered that a chipmunk had a burrow under the shrub and had found the inner workings of an old greeting card and was trying to drag it into its burrow, but every time it moved it, it played "New York, New York." Case closed! Guess the chipmunk will have to find another form of entertainment.

Are Blue Jays Good Engineers? Nope!

We have lived where we are now for over forty years. This happened at our house many years before I got into the pest control business. We live in a ranch house, and at the bedroom end of the house, I have a rain barrel that has the downspout from the gutters going into it. Overhanging this rain barrel is a lilac bush. We have a front porch on the house that has a railing on it. One

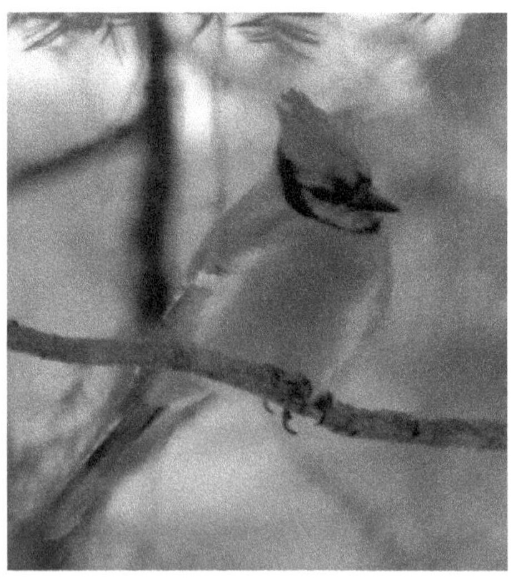

evening in May, my wife and I were watching the news in the living room at the other end of the house. Suddenly, there was a tremendous screeching coming from outside at the other end of the house. It continued for several minutes and was loud enough that I got up to go investigate. I went out the front door and walked to the end of the house, and in the lilac bush was a blue jay screaming its head off. They had built a nest in the lilac bush, mostly out of twigs, and it had fallen apart, dumping three baby blue jays into the full rain barrel. They did not even have any feathers yet. I scooped them out of the rain barrel, rebuilt the nest as best I could, and put the babies back in the nest. I did not hold out much hope that they would survive, being chilled like they were, from being in the water.

We went back to watching TV, and I forgot about it for a few days. A few days later, we were watching the news again, and suddenly, the blue jay was on the porch railing, looking at me through the window and screaming its head off again. I immediately got up, went outside to the porch, and the blue jay flew to the end of the house. I followed it, and yep, the babies were in the rain barrel again. I repeated the process, and there were no further episodes, so the babies were eventually successfully fledged. I am still amazed that that blue jay knew that I had helped it before, and when it happened again, it came looking for me to help it once more.

Just an FYI: You may have heard that if a human touches a baby bird, the parents will abandon the nest and they will die. That is an old wives' tale and is not true at all.

Nope, Can't Help You with That!

In my hometown, we have a large swampy area with a pond in the back of it. There is a spit of land running out through the center of it that someone built a house on. I do not know how they got around all the wetland regulations, but that is a question for another time. Anyway, I got a call from a woman who identified herself as the woman who owned that home. She told me that every summer, they have a major problem with big snapping turtles coming up on their lawn, digging holes, and laying their eggs. Was there anything that I could do to prevent this from happening? I mentally shook my head and thought, *This is a classic example of someone building in a wildlife habitat and then expecting humans to change the animal's behavior.*

I said to her as nicely as could, "Well, those turtles have been doing that since the end of the last ice age, and I doubt there is anything that can be done to prevent it. Unfortunately, you are just going to have to live with it and watch something that few people ever see."

Just a little sidenote on turtles. June is the month when turtles start breeding and laying eggs. They will go to historic spots to dig holes and lay eggs. Sometimes those spots involve crossing a road. If you see a turtle crossing a road, please stop and help it cross. They can be picked up by the side of their shell without harm. Just move them off the road in the direction they were headed. They will appreciate not being squashed by some vehicle.

Bird in the Wall?

This must be one of the funniest things that ever happened to me in my twenty-five years in the business.

A few years ago, my grandson had started working with me with the intent of taking over the business when I retired. Anyway, we were out doing jobs on a Monday and just finishing when I got a call from the caretaker at a local senior housing project where I had done work in the past (usually trapping and removing the raccoons with their young getting into the dumpsters in the May/June period)! Anyway, I told the guy we would be there shortly. Seems one of the residents had a bird in her wall, and the caretaker could not figure out how it got into it. We arrived and went to the unit. Sure enough, coming from the wall at the head of her bed was a "chirp, chirp, chirp" sound, the exact sound a bird would make! The woman said she had been hearing it on and off since late last week, so the bird would have to be able to get in and out, or it would have been dead long ago!

I stepped outside to check the roofline looking for any hole where the bird might get in and did not really see much. There was one spot, but that was a long shot. I did not hear any chirping either. I went back inside. There was the sound again! I went into the adjoining unit and heard nothing in a shared wall. Now if a bird were in the wall, don't you think you would hear it from both sides of the wall? I went back into the offending unit and started looking around. My grandson got down on his knees (I have trouble doing that anymore) and put his head under the little table that was being used as a nightstand. He said the noise was loud under there, so could it be a cricket under the dresser that was right next to the nightstand? I pulled out the dresser. Nothing! I pulled out the drawers. Still nothing! So I decided to pull out the drawer in the nightstand, and the sound got a lot louder. All three of us simultaneously saw the problem and said, "Hearing aids." The woman had put her hearing aids in a little bowl in the drawer without turning them off, and the noise was the hearing aids getting feedback from each other. Problem solved! So even though we deal mostly with critters, it is not always critters causing the problem!

Safety Issues

A lot of this business has to do with ladder work, crawling around people's roofs, attics, and crawl spaces, and encountering potentially dangerous animals in those areas.

Raccoons, which I dealt with many, many times are the number 1 carrier of rabies in Connecticut. I never had any exposure to it, so I am lucky that way, but it was always a concern. I did get preexposure rabies vaccine when I started the business.

The ladder work is in and of itself dangerous. One thing that happened to me will show how fast something can happen. I was at a "squirrel in the chimney" job and had set up my ladder to rest near the top of the chimney and was climbing up it. I had a rope to drop down the chimney because I could not get the squirrel out from inside the house. The chimney was one of the kinds that had four bricks on each corner and a piece of flagstone (or blue stone) resting on those four corners. I got near the top and had to grab one of those stacks of bricks on the corner. Now I thought they were mortared together and would be a good handhold. Nope! They were just stacked one on top of one another, and as I put my weight into my grab, the four bricks came right off, leaving that huge piece of flagstone sliding right toward my throat. Somehow, I was able to keep my composure and managed to get my hand on the edge of the bluestone and stop it and push it back so it was balanced on the other three corners. I went down and got the bricks from the corner that had fallen, brought them back up, and put the chimney back together.

That was very scary. If that bluestone had pushed me off the ladder, I would probably have been killed and likely decapitated.

One other thing that happened to me that did result in injury actually turned out to be quite fortunate. This happened in 2016. I was on my stepladder, trying to get into a guy's attic to put mouse bait up there. The stepladder collapsed and dumped me on the floor. I landed on the right side of my head and shoulder. The customer said I was out cold for about thirty seconds. I was taken to the hospital by ambulance. I was conscious but a little groggy. In the hospital, they did a CAT scan on me to make sure everything was okay inside. As I lay there with my wife and two daughters with me, the radiologist came in and said, "Do you know you have an ascending thoracic aortic aneurysm?" What! Well, turns out that there is a ballooning of my aorta right where it comes off my heart. I also tore my rotator cuff in my right shoulder, which required surgery. I already knew I had a partial tear that would have required surgery at some point anyway, so this just brought it front and center, and I got it taken care of. The discovery of the aneurysm was fortunate. Since it was discovered, I can now have it monitored to see if it reaches the danger point. (It was 4.5 centimeters, and they don't worry about them until they reach 5). As I write this book in 2024, I have had it checked every year, and it is still 4.5. Maybe I was just born with it.

Hope you have enjoyed this little book. I know I had fun for the twenty-five years I ran the business. Well, most of the time I did!

Thanks for reading!

About the Author

 Jon Quint is a lifelong resident of Woodbury, Connecticut. He attended Woodbury Schools and enrolled at Marietta College in Marietta, Ohio, in 1960. After two years at Marietta, he transferred to the University of Connecticut in Storrs, Connecticut, where he received a bachelor of arts degree with a major in geology.

He married in 1964 and had three daughters: Linda, Karla, and Kristen. He was divorced in 1981, and shortly thereafter, he married his current wife, Liz, and became stepfather to Matthew, Liz's son from her first marriage. They have been married for forty-two years.

He spent over thirty years in corporate America doing production planning work before being laid off several times, and in 1995, he decided he had had enough of working for other people and started North Forty Pest Control Co., LLC. In 2022, he retired, and sold the business to his grandson Jordan. He also kept honeybees for over thirty-five years, and at his peak, he had sixty-two hives.

He always liked to write, especially letters to the editor of the local newspaper. For a while, he authored two blogs: http://quint-essentialconservativeramblings.blogspot.com/ and http://nfpestcontrol.blogspot.com/.

He still lives in Woodbury with his wife, and this is his first book.